To:

....

From:

....

Louis Weber, CEO
Publications International, Ltd.
7373 North Cicero Avenue
Lincolnwood, Illinois 60712

ISBN-13: 978-1-4127-1578-2
ISBN-10: 1-4127-1578-4

Manufactured in China.

8 7 6 5 4 3 2 1

A Warm Cup of Kindness for FRIENDS™

WEST SIDE PUBLISHING

Contents

You Can't Live Without Them...

Every woman has something she should never do without. It's not a pair of black strappy heels or a subscription to a glossy fashion magazine. It's not a foolproof recipe for crème brûlée or a platinum-level credit card.

A woman's secret weapon is her girlfriends.

Girlfriends are part of what makes for a happy and fulfilling life. They are more useful than any wardrobe consultant, stronger than a four-dollar shot of espresso, and able to boost a friend out of the doldrums quicker than a pint of chocolate chunk ice cream. It's our friends who put us back together after a bad breakup and celebrate with us when we're on top of the world.

Girlfriends fill a variety of needs in our lives, and no two friends hold exactly the same place in our hearts. Some friends inspire us. Some challenge us. Some gal pals make us laugh while others simply listen. Some are once-in-a-while e-mail friends, and others are the first people we talk to every morning. Some gals we may have known since child-hood while others we met last week at the gym.

But our friends share one thing in common: they add color and warmth to our lives. *A Warm Cup of Kindness™ for FRIENDS* is a collection of stories that highlight these special relationships and the way they enrich our lives. No two stories are alike, just as no two friends on the phone's speed dial are exactly the same.

Reading through these short 'n sweet anecdotes is like hanging out with your girlfriends, swapping dating disasters, makeup tips, and career advice. See who comes to mind when you read a particular story—perhaps even call her up. Chat a bit; catch up. Thank her for being in your life; maybe even read her the story. After all, *A Warm Cup of Kindness™* is a lot like life: the best part is sharing it with a friend.

Who needs therapy?
I have girlfriends!

tell me all about it

In the Saddle

As the hot asphalt flew beneath our tires and the sun-spackled vineyards flew by, I knew that this trip was worth every sacrifice I'd made to get there. A three-day bicycle trip through California's wine country would be wonderful under any circumstances, but sharing it with my best friend made it that much more special.

Shannon and I met when we were both in our twenties and lived only a few miles apart. Seven years later, we now lived on opposite sides of the country. I had two children, and she had just started a new job and a new relationship. Our everyday lives didn't intersect any longer; catching up, even by phone, required juggling multiple personal schedules and time zones.

That's why a vacation together—away from our families and other responsibilities—was so appealing. We would have the chance to renew our friendship without distractions of crying babies or paperwork. Excited for our adventure, we packed our duffle bags and padded bike shorts and met in sunny California.

In the days preceding the trip, my anxiety started to bubble: What if my little ones didn't like staying at Grandma's house? What if Shannon and I ran out of things to talk about? What if she rode faster than I

did? What if the whole trip was a disaster? It was with more than a little trepidation that I met her plane, but as soon as she arrived, it was as if no time had passed. We immediately fell into our old rhythm of talking and laughing, and soon the excitement crept back in.

The following three days were full of sore muscles, sunburns, and miles of hot, dusty roads. The hours we spent riding side by side offered us a connection we hadn't had in years—one that I've experienced with few other people. We grew closer over hours spent gossiping and laughing, trading stories and jokes. Even the silences created a new intimacy for us, taking in the quiet roads and the splendor of our surroundings. We could have talked and laughed by e-mail or phone, but those deep, soul-touching silences can only be shared in person. And because we had both made an effort to be together, cycling in California, those moments were all the more special.

A Friend for Every Occasion

I think of my girlfriends the way I think about shoes. I don't mean my friends are disposable, easy to re-place, or shoved aside when I don't need them. What I mean is that I have a variety of friends just like I have a variety of footwear. And just as different shoes match different outfits, my various friends fit different aspects of my life.

I have my shopping friend, a divalicious buddy who is always up on the latest styles and won't hesitate to tell me if a skirt I've squeezed into makes me look a bit, well, plump. She's the one I grab when I need to find the perfect black dress for my husband's work party. I also have my crafty friend, who has a closet full of paints, glitter, scissors, and glue and will gladly help me cut out, stamp, and heat emboss 150 birth-announcement cards.

I have a dozen other ladies in my friendship closet, including my running friend, whom I count on when I need to burn off stress (and chocolate chip cookies); my book club girls, who give me recommenda-tions for the latest reads; my school-mom friends, who can cover the pick-up and drop-off of my children at a moment's notice if I'm caught

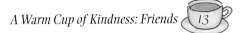

at work; and my spill-your-guts friend, to whom I tell my innermost thoughts (even the bad stuff) and she loves me anyway.

Over the years, I've learned that not having one single best friend is not just okay, it's wonderful! If I wore the same pair of shoes day in and day out, no matter how comfortable the shoes were, it would get a little monotonous—plus there's always the risk of wearing them out. But mixing things up and changing shoes every day means that I have just the right pair for each occasion. And best of all, just as with shoes, if you find a friend you can't live without, there's always room for more.

❧❧

Girlfriends are like a strong cup of coffee: They both pick you up and give you a jolt of energy when you need it most.

Together We Stand

"I have something to tell you..."

Carol's news of her breast cancer diagnosis darkened the mood of her weekly lunch with her best friends, Angie and Ro. The three women met each Thursday at the same café, usually to laugh and gossip—only today there wasn't much to laugh about.

Angie and Ro were as supportive as they could be, assuring Carol they would help her through anything and everything. Her lumpectomy went well, but then she was told she must also have chemotherapy. It was a process she dreaded.

Angie and Ro were there for each and every chemo treatment, trying their best to make Carol laugh, to keep her spirits up. The hair loss was especially hard for Carol to bear. She had always prided herself on her glossy, gorgeous hair. But soon her beautiful long locks fell out and Carol, embarrassed, hid her head under hats and scarves.

"Sorry, we've got stuff to do. But we'll see you later, okay?"

Carol hung up the phone. It was Thursday, but for the first time in years, Angie had called to say that she and Ro had to cancel. Carol always looked forward to their weekly visits, even if she felt weak and tired from the chemo treatments. She felt as if her friends were too busy to deal with her, and it hurt her feelings. For the first time since her diagnosis, she began to feel sorry for herself.

When her doorbell rang that evening, Carol discovered the reason for the last-minute cancellation. There stood her two best friends, both wearing big, bright hats, boldly decorated with ribbons and pins. "Ta-da!" sang Ro, grinning. Carol laughed and invited them inside. Once in the living room, Angie and Ro ceremoniously removed their hats. Underneath, they revealed their own freshly shaven heads.

Carol's jaw dropped. It seemed to take forever for her to find her voice. When she was finally able to speak, she found she didn't need to. Her eyes welling with tears, she hugged her friends tightly, stunned at their show of solidarity. It was that act more than anything else that made Carol feel strong and empowered.

Carol eventually went into remission, and her hair grew out into an adorable short shag. Ro and Angie let their hair grow out as well, and

when they were out together, people would often say they looked like sisters.

It must have been the hair.

Nothing heals life's bumps, breaks, and bruises better than the undivided attention of a good friend.

Mommies R Us

When I finally got around to having children, it seemed my friend-making days were pretty much behind me. I mean, when kids have to come first, it doesn't allow for a whole lot of "me-time," let alone the chance to nurture a friendship. While my fellow moms are fun to chatter with while our respective kids pound mulch into powder at the playground, in general, the friendships that I've made since becoming a mom seem to lack any real connection outside of our children. The moms—myself included—sit and talk about weather and school, food and errands, and which store has the best kids' clothes on sale. That's all well and good, but I didn't realize how much better it could be until I met Jennifer.

It began when the friendship between our sons evolved from school playground shenanigans to at-home playdates. That's when the true friendship magic began for me: Jennifer didn't merely want to drop off or pick up a kid or two, *she* wanted to play as well. Even more surprisingly, I found that her enthusiasm made me want to join in the fun! When we took our kids sledding, we didn't sip hot chocolate in the minivan while the children played—we beat them in the race down the hill. We didn't shy away from the chaos that is Chuck E. Cheese's; instead, we pried tokens out of our children's sticky little hands so that

we could compete with each other at the games.

Jennifer and I haven't been able to swing it yet, but we have high hopes of taking our kids to a concert. We will, no doubt, be in the thick of it—laughing, having fun, and dancing right along with our children.

I've always been open to life's little surprises, but my friendship with Jennifer is one of my most treasured relationships. And one day, when the kids have flown the nest, I bet you can imagine who I'll be calling when my hectic life once again permits the decadent pursuit of me-time!

❧❧

The relationships that I choose to nurture, in turn, nurture me every day of my life.

Coming Full Circle

Linda and Ree met in English class in high school, two book-loving girls who bonded like glue during those trying years. The two were inseparable—you could never find Linda without Ree, or vice versa. Even dating was easily managed: they just usually doubled.

The friends were brokenhearted when Linda's family moved to another town during their senior year. Although Linda and Ree stayed in contact for a while, distance eventually took its toll and the girls lost touch. Time passed, and years slipped into decades.

One day, Linda, who was back in town visiting friends, ran into Ree's mother. Linda got Ree's information and anxiously called her forgotten friend. As soon as Linda heard Ree's voice on the other end of the phone line, it was as if no time had passed. Although 20 years and a thousand miles lay between them, all distance vanished as the old friends laughed and reminisced about their high school days.

Linda spilled the news that she had gotten engaged a year ago, and Ree excitedly said she had as well. They began discussing their future spouses, and thought it rather amusing that both of their fiancés

had the last name of Burkett. The more they talked, the more it dawned on Linda and Ree that something really strange was going on.

As it turned out, both had met wonderful men who shared a number of similarities beyond their surname. In fact, their fiancés were first cousins! The two long-lost friends couldn't believe their amazing—if not eerie—luck. Not only had they found one another and rekindled their friendship, but now they would be family.

And so it happened that within a year, Linda and Ree married Rob and Jack in an extravagant double wedding. It was a magical day that none of them would ever forget, proving that friendship and love really do come full circle.

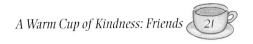

The best friendships mellow with age into a fine wine that soothes with just the right amount of sweetness.

Soap Sud Buds

Working with Julie on the special marketing project was driving Sandy crazy. Julie was one of those catty, bitter women who competed with everyone for the boss's attention. Sandy groaned when she thought about spending two months together with Julie in the same office.

In general, Sandy was lucky to have a job she loved; she got along with most of her colleagues, and she liked her boss. Julie was the only thorn in her side. Their first meeting to discuss preliminary ideas was tense and brief, with Julie railroading almost everything she wanted into the plan and ignoring anything Sandy had to offer. The second and third meetings went the same way, and Sandy was nearing a point where she'd have to tell her boss she wanted off the project.

One day as Sandy was getting lunch, she found Julie watching *Guiding Light* on the lunchroom TV and weeping. Alarmed, Sandy felt compelled to ask what was wrong. Julie sniffled and poured out stories of betrayal and divorce. It took Sandy a minute to realize Julie was talking about the soap opera and not real life.

Before too long, the women were meeting for lunch every day, watching their favorite soap. Together they laughed and cried over the antics of Reva, Josh, Harley, and Gus. Sandy began to look forward to their lunches together, and as the two women slowly became friends, their work took on a whole new mood.

One day, Julie opened up to Sandy, confiding in her about her recent divorce. Like a scene from a soap opera, Julie's husband had left her for one of his work colleagues, and it had left Julie feeling bitter and hostile toward other women. Sandy listened with compassion, and it seemed to change something in Julie—she began to be more trusting, less competitive, and more lighthearted.

Eventually, their *Guiding Light* fan club grew to six women. A friendship blossomed over their shared love of soap operas, and the women discovered in the process that they had other things in common as well. For Sandy, it meant coming to work each day looking forward to a project she had once felt like quitting.

Who knows if Reva and Josh will end up together, but Sandy and Julie are friends for life.

In Search of Same (ISOS)

These days, you can find anything from a nanny to a dog-walker to a husband on the Internet. So why is it that people don't advertise on the Internet when they're looking for other types of relationships; for instance, friends? Imagine how much easier life would be if you could just post an online ad stating the truth: that you're feeling a little lonely and are looking for a like-minded girlfriend to share celebrity gossip, gooey chocolate desserts, and heart-to-heart talks.

To meet this need, I advocate the creation of a site for gals in search of pals to hook members up with compatible girlfriends. Of course, we'd need to develop our own criteria for our site. Forget about the height,

weight, and occupation data a typical singles ad includes—that stuff is pretty much irrelevant for girlfriends. Instead shoe size, shopping preference (mall vs. online, upscale vs. discount), and favorite movies would be among the critical elements for our profiles.

Our Web site would have all the usual acronyms used in singles sites, but they'd be tailored to our specific needs: "BYOB" now means "Bring Your Own Baby," while someone who enjoys adventurous dining experiences is an "EOE," or "Equal Opportunity Eater." On our site, "FDIC" would refer not to financial insurance, but to "Friends Desired for Intense Chatting."

Instead of posting pictures of ourselves sucking in guts and cheekbones, we'll include photos of our closets. After all, if we both own ten pairs of flip-flops and absolutely no heels, we're bound to get along, right? We could even note the kind of car we drive—not to be snobby, but to see if there are carpooling prospects. The mommies could include the ages of their kids, rather than their own age.

So if you are online and see an ad that reads, "MF ISOS. BYOB, EOE, FDIC. 10YO, 7YO, 3YO. 7.5 shoe, Sleepless in Seattle," accompanied by a photo of a closet of sweats and jeans, you'll know that's me.

Drop me a line. Who knows? Maybe we'll become BFF (Best Friends Forever).

❧❧

Friends fill in the blanks for you.

Spreading the Warmth

Running her own home design business left Rita with little time for much of anything else—even her social life was at a standstill.

She got a phone call from her old college friend Sammie, who announced she would be in Rita's neighborhood for a job interview. She invited Rita out to lunch, and at first, Rita's instinct was to say she was just too busy. It wasn't really a lie, after all. But guilt got the better of her, and she met her friend at a local café. It had been months since they'd last talked, and they had a lot to catch up on. As Rita listened, Sammie filled her in about her volunteer work at a nonprofit agency dealing with several charities for the poor and homeless.

Sammie's obvious passion for her volunteer work was contagious. Rita found herself listening intently to Sammie's stories of the people she helped and how the work made her feel fulfilled.

Rita felt oddly jealous—her business was growing, as well as her bank account, but it felt as though other parts of her life were empty. She had never been much for giving to others; not because she wasn't a caring person, but she was just too busy. She explained this to Sammie, and before Rita could protest, Sammie made her agree to come down to the homeless shelter that weekend to help at the soup kitchen. Rita sputtered about scheduling conflicts, while Sammie just grinned.

At the shelter, Rita felt uncomfortable and out of place, but Sammie showed her around and introduced her to the rest of the volunteer staff. Before long, Rita was serving breakfast and chatting with the local homeless folks, befriending them and listening to their stories. Sammie smiled as she saw how her old friend glow with a new energy—Rita was a natural and never knew it.

The day was long, but Rita had to admit that she felt better and more relaxed than she had in years. Something had shifted inside her, and she felt a sense of purpose and connection that her high-octane life had never given her.

"You know, Sammie, I really hope you get that job," said Rita, as they washed dishes together.

"Oh yeah? Why's that?" asked Sammie.

"I have a feeling spending more time with you is just what I need."

As unique as they may be on the outside,
friends are kindred spirits on the inside;
soul companions walking together
on the path of life.

Coming Together

When my husband asked for a divorce, I found myself riding an emotional roller coaster. Some days I felt like all I could do was hang on and hope for the best.

What bothered me almost as much as the loss of my marriage was the thought of losing the friends that Paolo and I had made as a couple. Church friends, neighbors, couples we had known since our idealistic college days—I worried that they would feel they had to side with either Paolo or me and, frankly, that mine might not be the side they would choose.

After the divorce, it quickly became clear to me that my son, Jonah, and I would do better if we moved away from old memories and got a fresh start in a new house. I approached our neighbor, Carol, to be our real estate agent, though I was a little hesitant because Paolo and I had spent many an evening with her and her husband, Ted. To my relief, no choosing of sides was necessary; Carol asked no questions about the divorce. "I'm going to miss having you as a neighbor, but we'll always stay in touch," she said, hugging me. "And your instincts are right: fresh house, fresh start."

While I went with Carol to look at houses, Ted took Jonah to the movies or had him over to shoot hoops. Carol helped me find the perfect cottage but refused to talk about discussing her fee until I was back on my feet. When our church family learned about the move, Alice—a brusque older woman from my Sunday school class—put together a moving crew. She even organized a potluck at her house for the movers and waved away my profuse thanks. "Gotta feed people," she said matter-of-factly.

I loved our new home, but it needed work. The week after we moved in, I heard from James and Beth, college friends that I hadn't seen in years. They offered to come over and help me paint. I'll never forget what a welcome sight they made coming up the walk, Beth gaily brandishing her tools. "This is the end-all of paint rollers, I'll have you know!" she boasted, a big grin lighting up her face.

While I wouldn't wish divorce on anyone, it brought me an unexpected blessing: I learned how many true friends I have.

No, Actually—I Don't!

Lisa was two days away from the biggest event of her life.

Her stomach was knotted with anxiety, but her friends and family told her it was just excitement, or perhaps just a touch of cold feet. After all, in two days she would be married.

But Lisa knew in her heart that her subconscious was trying to tell her something, something she didn't want to face. She felt an enormous pressure—so many people were waiting for this event. Even her best friend through high school, Vi, was coming to stay with her before the wedding. They'd stayed in casual contact over the years, sending birthday and holiday cards with quickly written updates. While Lisa was looking forward to seeing her old friend, she just didn't feel up to entertaining her.

When Vi arrived, she bustled about the apartment, taking control and forcing Lisa to relax. On their first night together, instead of reminiscing about the past or getting excited about the future, Lisa broke down and began to cry.

Vi got up and sat near her; again, in her usual Vi fashion, she asked the direct question that Lisa herself had been avoiding.

"Is this marriage what you really want?"

The directness of the question brought Lisa's tears to a halt. Over the next five hours and a bottle of wine, the two women talked honestly and openly about Lisa's feelings and thoughts of the future. Vi had a way of bringing out the truth without judgment, and Lisa finally admitted that while she loved her fiancé, it was not the kind of love that would sustain a marriage.

Although she knew her decision would hurt people, that night Lisa realized she could not go through with the wedding. Vi encouraged her to do what was best for herself, with love and compassion for everyone involved.

"But Vi, I'm scared. I don't want to hurt anyone. I don't want to disappoint anyone. How do I go through with this?" asked Lisa.

"Oh, hush," Vi said, hugging Lisa close, "you're not disappointing anyone. Listen, you only have one life. This is not a dress rehearsal—this is the real deal. So live!"

Lisa knew her friend was right, and with Vi's encouragement and advice, she was able to gather the strength to end her relationship and call off the wedding. She vowed that one day she would be there for her friend, just as Vi had been there for her.

Rock 'n Roll Mamas

Mia and Loren met in high school and had stayed close over the years. As Loren's 50th birthday approached, Mia decided she couldn't think of a better surprise for her best friend than two tickets to a Rolling Stones concert. Sure, they were respectable, mature ladies, but wasn't the latest saying that 50 was the new 40?

When Mia presented Loren with the tickets, Loren acted shocked. "You've got to be kidding! Us? At a Stones concert?" she said, eyes twinkling. "We'll throw out a hip or something!" Like two high school girls, they spent the next week deciding what to wear, sorting through their closets, and hitting the local mall.

Even decked out in jeans and Stones T-shirts, they felt a bit out of place at the concert—at first glance everyone seemed so young. But as the crowd grew, Mia and Loren noticed more than half the attendees were at least in their 40s. With the pressure of youth out of the way, they began to relax and have fun.

When the music began, any question of age or appropriateness went right out the window as the two "respectable, mature ladies" jumped

out of their seats, screaming and singing along to the songs they had both grown up with. When the concert was over, they were tired from dancing, but glowing and happy.

On the way home from the concert, Loren thanked Mia for the tickets and for reminding her that she was as young in her heart as she felt—which at that moment was pretty young. In fact, Loren was feeling so feisty and energetic that she suggested they stop off at a local hot spot, where the two spent the next two hours singing karaoke to all their favorite songs.

That night, Loren and Mia promised they would do something crazy and fun on a regular basis—not just to remind themselves of their inner youth, but to celebrate their friendship and love for each other.

Next up: Vegas!

꧁꧂

Pencil in appointments with acquaintances, but ink in dates with friends.

Girlfriends are like chocolate, automatic transmissions, and indoor plumbing: We only know how much we need them when we try to live without them.

Whispers of Wisteria

"Remission" was a bittersweet word. But when Deanna sang it over the phone to the tune of *The Mickey Mouse Club* theme song, I realized that she had chosen to see her time between treatments—and relapses—as a reprieve and not as a stay of execution.

We had been best friends since college and had celebrated our 30th year as friends last July at a spa in Denver, halfway between our homes in Maryland and Oregon. Now between her medical bills and my children's tuition, we were as broke as we had been as undergraduates. Although I could practically hear my credit card cracking in two, I told her I was on my way to Maryland to celebrate her remission. We would stay in a motel with a hot tub, which was as close to a spa as we could afford.

While searching online for the best motel rates, I remembered our old friend Margie. After college, we had lost contact with her. She was the one who kept a fresh bouquet of wisteria, "pruned" from the park, in the roach-infested apartment we all shared as undergraduates. As a joke, she would leave the bouquet of flowers prominently displayed with an attached gift card reading "All my love, Joe." Thanks to the fictitious Joe, we learned that men are fiercely competitive and would often step up

their own attentions toward us. What we loved about Margie was her ability to find humor in every situation. At the spa we had committed to finding Margie, but Deanna got sick again, and Margie slipped off the radar.

I charged three nights at a motel with a Jacuzzi, but before I shut off my computer, I ran some search programs. While I did not find Margie, I managed to locate several college friends, one of whom knew enough about Margie for me to find her. Margie said that although she was in Texas and was as broke as we were, she would still love to join us.

The motel turned out to be completely run-down, and the Jacuzzi smelled like a chemical vat, but when we saw Margie through the steam, we burst out laughing. She was carrying an armload of wisteria she said she had pruned from her yard. "Alright, y'all—we're in this together!" she yelled, and jumped in the hot tub with all her clothes on.

Deanna was nearly rolling on the ground, laughing. It was so good to see her in high spirits again. As I picked up the bouquet of wisteria and set it on a nearby table, I knew our friendship was stronger than ever.

No Time for Pity

Normally Becca loved celebrations of any kind—if there was a reason to party, she was there—but with the arrival of her fortieth birthday, she was uncharacteristically depressed. "C'mon, honey. Let's plan a party for you," said her husband, Graham.

"Nope. I'm sitting this one out," Becca said, shaking her head. "No party, no presents, no cake. Can't we just pretend this one isn't happening?"

In the week leading up to her birthday, Becca had been thinking about all the goals she had hoped to achieve by this age. She slumped a bit at how it seemed she had only made a small dent in her list of aspirations.

It was a good start, sure, but only a start. Self-doubt began to creep into other areas of her life; suddenly she found herself leaning into the bathroom mirror, examining the fine etching of lines around her mouth. Becca knew her moping was a little ridiculous, but she couldn't help feeling that the only celebration she wanted to have was a pity party— all by herself.

The day of her birthday Becca was suspiciously wondering whether there would be a surprise party in the works after all. To her relief, there wasn't: While Graham was being especially kind to her, he took her at her word and was acting as if it were an ordinary day. By evening,

though, Becca began to second-guess her request. She had made such a big deal of the drama of aging that it felt like others should acknowledge it too. *Maybe I messed this one up*, she mused. *A little bit of recognition would have been nice!*

Just as Becca was making a cup of birthday coffee for herself, the doorbell rang. Her best friend, Lindsey, poked her head in the door, brandishing a brightly colored paper rolled up and tied like a scroll. "Don't be mad!" Lindsey begged Becca. "It isn't a present, and it isn't a cake—it's just a card. And you didn't say no *cards!*"

Becca beamed and hugged her surprised friend, who was expecting a different reaction. Cups of coffee in hand, they sat down to read the card, which listed the reasons why Lindsey loved Becca—one reason for each year of her life. All the big things were there, as well as the little things: the way Becca dropped everything to be there for a friend, the way she cranked up the music on her car radio and sang along, her fierce determination.

Becca re-rolled the card, tears of gratitude streaming down her face. It was then that she realized that she had had a very good life so far. With her husband's love and a wonderful friend like Lindsey, the best was yet to come.

Friends don't see the walls we
put up around ourselves;
they find the doors and walk right in.

Quiet Compassion

It was like this: I was the outgoing one, Chrissy was the shy one. We would never have met in high school if we hadn't been assigned to share a locker. Since she never made a fuss, I didn't know what a wonderful artist Chrissy was until I saw her sketches tacked up in our locker. Right there on paper, she had transformed our high school into a fantasyland, her favorite teacher drawn as a benevolent queen. She blushed when I told her how good they were. "Just doodles," she murmured, obviously pleased.

Both Chrissy's friends and mine were surprised as she and I became closer. I was a cheerleader, and although Chrissy was too tactful to say so, I suspected that in her friends' eyes that automatically made me a snob. Of course, my own friends were no better, rolling their eyes at what they thought were the boring, mousy girls.

My little world crashed when my boyfriend broke up with me right before the homecoming dance. My friends were sympathetic but too busy with dance preparations to give me their time. Feeling alone, I called Chrissy, whom I'd seldom seen outside of school.

"I just don't know what to do," I sobbed over the phone.

"Let me come sit with you," she suggested. She showed up at my house with her sketchpad, and soon I was laughing at her caricature of my

ex-boyfriend. That evening spent doodling and giggling cemented our friendship.

Over the years, I lost track of most of my high school friends. But not Chrissy. When my father was ill, other friends asked if there was anything they could do, but Chrissy came right away to lend her support. We didn't talk much, but she stayed with me for hours as night fell in the hospital; her presence calmed me greatly.

A few years ago, I went into labor with my first child while my husband was out of town. Babies don't necessarily arrive when convenient, and when my water broke at midnight, I called Chrissy, who again met me at the hospital. Huffing and crying, I grabbed her hand after one big contraction. "I'm not sure I can do this," I whined.

"Yes, you can," she said. She sat with me all night, softly repeating those three words.

"Hey, I thought I was supposed to be the cheerleader!" I gasped at one point, flashing her a pained smile.

When my husband arrived early in the morning, Chrissy slipped away to let us have our private time. The baby was a girl, and we named Chrissy as her godmother. Not only did I want to honor my friend, but I also hoped that her gift of empathy will rub off on my precious little girl.

Droppin' By

My family had just moved to a new state, and so far it wasn't sitting well with me. Since I worked from home and didn't know how to begin making friends, I became quite lonely. Burying myself in work, I rarely ventured out into the world. One warm spring evening, I sat on the deck to watch my son play. It was lovely out-side, and many of my neighbors were walking, gardening, and mowing lawns. Their children played nearby, laugh-ing and screaming as they chased one another. Our neighborhood seemed to come alive after the hard Kansas winter.

I chatted idly on the phone as I watched my son, Thompson, play, and it took me a moment to notice a group of people walking across my back lawn. Barely glancing at them, I thought they were taking a shortcut through my yard, since all our yards were connected. Soon my deck was filled with neighbors of all ages: parents, kids, and teenagers. They all gathered in front of me.

One woman introduced herself as my next-door neighbor, Clara, and told me they had all dropped by to say hello. Her son was Thompson's age, and together the two boys eagerly ran off to play on the lawn. Tears filled my

eyes—this was a wish granted,
a hope becoming reality.

Soon everyone was milling around the
deck and yard, visiting with one another. I felt an immediate connection with
Clara; her act of reaching out to me,
to us, filled me with joy. She was kind,
generous, and funny, and we talked
while our children got to know each
other. I felt a friendship blooming—not
just for me, but for my son as well.

Over time, Clara proved to be a kindred spirit and the friend I had been
longing for. She confided that she had been waiting for a friend like me,
too. Our kitchen windows face each other, and it is a comfort knowing
she is right there when I need her. Having a friend so close by has been a
gift, and for the first time since moving, I finally feel like I am home.

❧❧

*Having a best friend is like
owning a diary that talks back.*

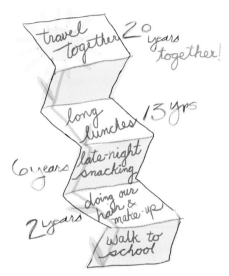

travel together 20 years together!

long lunches 13 yrs

6 years late-night snacking

2 years doing our hair & make-up

walk to school

You don't pick your friends so much as they find you. You don't create friendship so much as it unfolds naturally.

Merrym's Song

I love her and admire her more than any woman I know.

Merrym is in her late thirties and is in a wheelchair after suffering a stroke while still in her twenties. Talking is difficult for her and so is using her hands, and yet she talks and uses her hands more than anyone else—that's the kind of spirit she has. She is currently in a nursing home recovering from surgery. She is by far the youngest person there, and I know she is isolated; she must be lonely.

One day Merrym called and told me she wanted to show me something. I agreed to come by, but somehow the day got away from me. One errand turned into several and the hours slid by as a snowstorm hit town. Seeing cars off the road in several places, I told my husband I thought we should go home—we could see Merrym some other time. Giving me a look that told me I was being a lousy friend, he said we were going as promised.

The whole family crowded into Merrym's small room, our arms filled with fast food bags and drinks. The look of sheer joy on her face as she sat in her wheelchair, waiting, made my throat catch—to think that I had almost let her down!

"Yay!" she cried, greeting us with open arms. She is so loving, so jubilant; being greeted by Merrym is like walking into springtime.

She reached down by her wheelchair to turn on her CD player. It seemed like it, too, had been waiting for us to arrive.

Merrym had been learning a song in sign language as a gift to my son Noah, who is deaf, and had been patiently waiting all day to 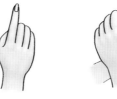 perform her song for us. Now I felt like an even bigger jerk.

Sweet and soothing music filled the room. As I watched her sign the song, my eyes welled with tears. It was truly beautiful. She signed with all her heart, her fingers stiff and unbending. The children were mesmerized while I sat in silence, tears pouring down my face. It was a magical, unforgettable moment.

She looked just like an angel. When the song finished, I leapt up, sobbing, to wrap my arms around her.

My dear friend had given us a beautiful, selfless gift, and I hope I can return the favor for her many times over.

As the Romans Do

"I'll never see Rome again," sighed my friend Anne. She was newly widowed, and Rome had been "their" city. She couldn't face it alone, she said. Though I'm not a big fan of cities—my dream of a perfect European vacation had always included lazing along the Riviera—I promised that when she was ready, I would go to Rome with her.

Months later, Anne called and I was pleased to hear the excitement in her voice. That is, until she said we would go to Rome that summer. You see, I hadn't really expected she'd take me up on my offer. Now there was no turning back; I couldn't disappoint her. I complained to my family about the chaos of urban life but got no sympathy. "You promised," my son said.

I packed comfortable shoes for the miles we would hike between the Vatican and the Forum and up and down Rome's seven hills. Anne, of course, was too thrilled to notice my grumpy mood as we arrived in Italy. From the taxi window, she excitedly pointed out the Colosseum and the many Renaissance buildings. With a small sigh, I realized that Rome's fountains were the closest I was going to get to a beach.

After we unpacked, she announced it was time for gelato. I asked her to explain.

"Ice cream," she said.

"I don't like ice cream."

She ignored me, and later as I licked drips of lemon gelato from my fingers, I asked her how many times a day we could have gelato. We agreed to a twice-daily occurrence.

Despite my initial resistance, that was the beginning of my love affair with Rome. The ancient buildings fascinated me, and the art ignited my imagination. And the food! I don't mind walking miles of cobblestone lanes in order to shed pasta pounds.

This year marked our seventh annual trip to Rome. Typically Anne and I traveled together; by now we had a series of shops and restaurants that were our favorite haunts. Each vacation spent exploring our favorite city brought us closer together. We even know each other's habits. I know she loves to hit the markets for supplies and snacks immediately upon arriving in town. She knows I like to take it slow and indulge in a lazy afternoon nap. But what we both share is a love for our daily gelato stops, marking a bond forged long ago.

Life is just so much more fun and fulfilling when you spend it in the company of friends.

An Extended Family

I had recently moved to a small Midwestern town and was fairly friendless. Everyone seemed to have known each other for years, and their social networks had long been established. Still, I remained pretty busy, juggling work, marriage, and two small children. I met my neighbors, who were nice and all, but I didn't feel like I really clicked with anyone in particular.

When I was casually introduced to a woman named Denise, it didn't strike me as a terribly momentous occasion. I'm sure I said, "Nice to meet you," or something equally ordinary, and thought that would be that. A week later, however, we started what would become our monthly lunches together.

Now, I'm not exactly an easygoing kind of gal. In fact, I'm more of a "How much can I possibly accomplish on my ever-expanding to-do list, needs-to-take-a-chill-pill" kind of gal. But there I was, at a table in the window of a little Italian restaurant the first Monday of every month. For two years, Denise and

I would eat pasta and share all the details of our lives prior to crossing paths.

Our lunches would often last for hours, approaching precariously close to dinnertime. Eventually, Denise enlisted her teenage son to help with my little ones so that we could continue our babbling, laughter-laced talks without limiting ourselves to the confines of the clock.

Somewhere along the line we brought my husband as well as her new beau and his son into our fold, and that was when the true magic of our friendship began. Lunches were replaced with family-style gatherings. Sometimes we even have sleepovers when no one wants to allow something as boring as  sleep to end the fun. Denise's mother, Grandma Doris, now joins us for themed dinners and game nights. You should see her belt out karaoke!

I can't imagine a holiday going by without spending time with these people who have become our closest and dearest friends. Our new makeshift family shares no bloodlines but knows no boundaries.

The Uplifters

There was nothing like a motivational seminar to get Melinda back on track, and fortunately her workplace offered several seminars per year. Each time she attended one, she left feeling more focused and clear about her goals and her dreams—none of which involved staying in her job as a realtor.

This seminar was much like the others that Melinda had been to, and as she scanned the audience, she noticed that the woman next to her seemed very intent on the lecturer. She had seen the woman on occasion at another local realty office, and so during the break she introduced herself. It turned out that Rachel was also a realtor, and as they sipped their coffee Rachel confessed that her goal was to get out of the business and do something more meaningful with her life—something that would inspire others and make her feel like she was being of service. Melinda was struck by how closely Rachel's goals matched her own, and the two went to lunch together, excitedly discussing their dreams and aspirations.

When they went back to the lecture hall, the speaker's topic was about having passion for your work. Melinda and Rachel listened as they were instructed to follow their heart and not be afraid to take risks. After the seminar, the two women went to dinner and continued talking about their lives. They had a lot in common, from their professions to their love of old classic movies, but especially their desire to inspire and motivate others.

"I want to be the person we look up to. I want to uplift others, make them see their potential," said Melinda.

"Oh, I've thought about it, I guess. I'd love to do it, but it never seemed to be a realistic profession," mused Rachel.

"Well, why not?" asked Melinda, grinning.

Inspired, the two women decided to take a life coaching course together, get their certification, and open their own company dedicated to making dreams come true. They decided to name their motivational company after their primary goal: Uplift. It took hard work, but within three years they were able to quit their real estate jobs entirely and devote all their time to their expanding business.

Neither Rachel nor Melinda minded the trials of starting a new business. Together, they were making other people's dreams come true, and in the process, making their own come true as well.

I don't have a personal trainer, but I do have a personal cheerleader—my best friend.

Wise Words

Brittany was about to be married, and frankly, she was more than a little nervous. Seeking advice, she confided in her mother's best friend, whom she called "Auntie Marnie." Auntie Marnie listened and comforted the bride-to-be. "Honey, don't worry. Just show up at the bridal tea party next week," she said.

At the party, Brittany expected the usual pre-wedding chitchat and party games and was surprised when Auntie Marnie distributed a pile of pastel index cards to the guests. "Now I want each of you to give our lovely bride your best piece of marital advice," she instructed. At first the women looked at each other, stumped, but soon they began to scribble away.

Aunt Marnie gathered the finished cards into a ribboned basket and gave them to Brittany to read aloud. Brittany was surprised at the wide array of answers, and as she read, the women chimed in with their opinions.

"Don't go to bed mad."

"Eat dinner together every night as a family."

"Always treat each other with respect."

Finally Brittany was at the last card. Looking closer, she recognized Auntie Marnie's familiar oversize, loopy handwriting. Her advice was, "Hang on to your girlfriends."

The younger women in the group were puzzled. "I thought we were supposed to write about love and marriage," said Brittany's friend Alicia. The older women in the group smiled in recognition.

"You don't want to put all of your emotional eggs in your husband's basket. That's too much of a burden on him!" said one.

"No matter how close you are to your husband, there are things that only another woman can understand," another pointed out.

"Your husband is never going to get it about shoes," someone else said, grinning.

"There's no teacher like experience," Auntie Marnie said knowingly. "If you use your girlfriends as a sounding board when difficulties arise, you'll probably make a better wife."

Brittany's anxiety lessened considerably. Auntie Marnie was right: Throughout the years, Brittany realized that by making it a priority to spend time with her friends, she had a much healthier marriage.

Sisters in Chocolate

 Every woman knows the value of chocolate. And I know many a woman who has certain friends she considers her "sisters in chocolate." At 42, I find that my most cherished friends and I all possess the same all-encompassing belief: that none of us could get through life without each other—or delicious chocolate.

Over the years, my friends and I have found that the answer to most of life's problems and stresses can usually be alleviated with morsels of sweet chocolate. End of a relationship? Send chocolate. Car problems? Chocolate. Depressed, lonely, stressed to the gills? Chocolate, chocolate, chocolate.

I can't see a Hershey's bar without thinking of Geneva, a longtime friend who signs all her letters with "Hugs and chocolate, Geneva." It always makes me smile. She is a maniac for chocolate; I think that the Hershey's factory must be her idea of paradise.

My pal Sandi is a true chocoholic like me. We don't nibble away at a candy bar, rewrapping it to enjoy later. Oh no, we will snarf down whatever chocolate we have on hand until it's gone. To us, there's no saving or sharing—only attacking until there is nothing left but the crumpled remains of the wrapper. Sandi has the same joyous, gleeful lust for chocolate that I do. Sometimes I think that if you cracked our heads open, truffles would fall out.

Among all of my chocolate-loving friends, Jane is the one who understands my adoration for chocolate like no other. She sends me sweets-themed gifts for every holiday: One year I received a crystal candy dish shaped like a chocolate kiss and filled with treats. I now keep my jewelry in it, and every time I put on earrings, I get an inexplicable craving for chocolate. Another brilliant gift was a chocolate fondue machine, which now sits in my cupboard, scarred and battered. With that old soldier I have drenched everything in chocolate, from fruit and graham crackers to brownies and cookies.

My dearest friends are my sisters in chocolate, connected by years of friendship, and we have always been there for one another. We simply couldn't get through life without each other...and chocolate.

❧❧

A true friend gives you half of her chocolate bar. The bigger half.

A good friend gives the best advice:
not necessarily what you want to
hear, but what you need to know.

Karaoke Queens

Jamie hated karaoke. It just seemed so cheesy and silly. The truth was, after breaking up with her longtime boyfriend, she didn't want to do much of anything that didn't include her couch and the TV.

In an effort to cheer her up, her friends Anna and Rae insisted she go out to the local karaoke bar with them. Jamie put up a good fight, but in the end she had no choice but to go along. Her friends could be relentless when they wanted something! The bar was packed and all around her people were having a good time, which only made Jamie feel worse. *I just want to go home and watch a good tearjerker on TV,* she thought to herself. But just as she was formulating her official "good excuse" for going home early, she was dragged onstage with her friends.

Anna chose the music, and Jamie cringed when she heard the opening notes to Gloria Gaynor's "I Will Survive," the classic post-break-up song. The girls started to sing and Jamie did her part, mumbling along listlessly. Then Rae shoved the mic over to Jamie, forcing her to go solo. Jamie wasn't sure what happened—whether it was the music or the lights, or maybe she was just tired of being sad—but as all eyes were on her, she began to belt out the song with passion.

There was just one problem: Jamie had the worst voice anyone had ever heard. Still, the audience began hooting and yelling, urging her on despite her inability to hold a note. When the crowd yelled for an encore, Jamie chose Dolly Parton's "I Will Always Love You"—the worst song for a terrible singer to attempt. The crowd ate it up.

When Jamie's throat finally gave out, she left the stage and headed toward the table where her friends were waiting with big smiles on their faces. She couldn't wait to thank them for getting her out of her house and out of her shell. On the way to the table, an attractive blond man with sparkling green eyes stopped Jamie.

"That was the worst singing I've ever heard in my life," he said, grinning. He introduced himself as Pete and offered to buy her a drink.

Five years later, when she and Pete were happily married and expecting their first child, Jamie would always get a kick out of telling the story of the worst—and the best—pick-up line she had ever heard.

Out of the Cold

Finally, I had enough frequent-flier miles to escape a Chicago winter. Every year I stave off frostbite while keeping the thermostat down to an affordable degree. But this winter was different: As November blew in with a blizzard, I was shoveling snow and smiling, knowing that in January I would be lounging on a Jamaican beach. Anticipation would get me through the holidays. Memories would keep my spirit toasty until the forsythia bloomed.

I was stomping snow off my boots when the phone rang. It was Beth, who had been my best friend for the 20 years she had lived in Chicago. As single women, we helped each other through the shoals of other people's expectations—specifically, why weren't we married yet? Even after she moved to Canada, we still told each other things only best friends do, like the real reason we weren't married: No one had asked us. I was eager to tell her about Jamaica, but I waited to hear why she had phoned.

She invited me to visit her. Now, why would she invite me to Montreal in January "for no particular reason" and then sound so hurt when I

refused? She knew how I hated winter. I hung up the phone, confused.

Over the next month, I enthusiastically readied myself for Jamaica. I rushed through my Christmas shopping, paying little attention to the gifts I hastily bought. While wrapping Beth's gift, I was struck with my selfishness. Beth had always been there when I needed her and had always called when she read a problem between the lines of an e-mail.

With a sigh, I changed the destination on my tickets: good-bye, Jamaica; hello, Montreal.

There was a good reason for Beth's caginess: She wanted to introduce me in person to Suchita, her adopted daughter from India. Beth glowed with love for her little girl; she wasn't so dour about being single any longer. Watching the two of them interact, seeing Beth's happiness and Suchita's childish wonder, inspired me. The next November, I bundled Nirmila, my own adopted daughter, into a snowsuit. Outside we built a snowman, and I pulled her through the neighbor-hood on her new sled. Her delight warmed me more than a hundred summer suns. With such a lively little girl to love, winter was now an exciting season. Thanks to Beth and my life-changing trip to Montreal, I had finally learned how to live and not just slog through every season of my life.

Crafty Kinship

In this increasingly Internet-savvy age, there are still some people who don't consider those who you've met online "real" friends. I couldn't disagree more whole-heartedly: Why should face-to-face time be a requirement of friendship?

My online group of craft friends is a good example. After five years together, we have discovered that the shared love of crafts that initially brought us together is actually low on the list of the ties that bind us. Deep down, we know that there isn't one of us who wouldn't drop everything to be there for the others.

The group founder is a friend of mine who encouraged me to join, even though I am, shall we say, "craft-challenged." But I dove in, and soon I found myself learning all sorts of new tricks and techniques. From the very beginning, we've shared other aspects of our lives. New babies mean baby shower gifts arriving by mail. When one of us becomes ill, the others flood her mailbox with cards and gifts until she's well. Milestones in each other's lives are celebrated by all of us. We pray for each other and rejoice in the highlights of life together.

Our friendship extends beyond the computer screen—sometimes we'll check in on one another with a phone call.

We have regular "swaps," where we each make themed crafts and then mail them to the other members of our group. One theme featured recipe books, made by sending a page to each member to put into her book. Those recipe books are my favorites; I cherish what they represent, as each page is as beautiful and unique as the woman who made it. Every homemade page reminds me what a big part of my life those ladies are.

The friendships I have found within this group are strong and enrich my life. Over the years, we have learned to lean on each other and have forged a bond that none of us expected from an online group. No matter

what anyone else says, these friendships are real, and I cannot imagine my life without them. These women may live in different zip codes, but they are the sisters of my heart.

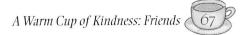

A true friend may
live in another state or
even another country,
but is always only a
heartbeat away.

Third Grade Now and Forever

Beth was the new girl in school, another third-grader to whom I was assigned as a "buddy." It was my job to make the new girl feel welcome and help her make friends.

I found out she lived only two blocks from me and we quickly became best friends, spending every day after school and every weekend together. We roller-skated, had sleepovers, and wrote each other notes at school. We were inseparable that year, as close as sisters. When Beth's family moved to another town the following summer, it broke our hearts, but we made a promise to remain friends forever.

We wrote and called for a few years, but as often happens with childhood friendships, we eventually lost touch. I thought of her often over the years, and I wondered where she lived, what her life was like, and whether she remembered me. I never forgot Beth, and I never had another friendship quite as close as ours.

When I was in my early twenties, I was visiting my mom at my childhood home. It just happened to be a rare, not-too-hot summer day, so

my sister and I decided to sit on the porch and chat. As we sat, I saw two young women walking across the street. Something seemed familiar about one of them, and I could see her glancing at me repeatedly as they passed. Soon they turned the corner and were gone.

A few minutes later I heard my mother's phone ring. She yelled that it was for me.

I knew the voice in an instant: older, yet the same. "Susan? This is Beth! Do you remember me?"

It was Beth and her sister I had seen earlier walking on my street! They were back in town visiting relatives. She came right over, and we spent hours talking and laughing, just like we did in the third grade. Time melted away, and our connection was as strong as ever.

I never would have dreamed that an accidental meeting would reunite me with my childhood best friend. Together again at last, we discovered that true friends could pick up where they left off, no matter what.

❧❧

Be the friend you would like to have.

What's in a Name?

Jennifer's diagnosis was a common one for pregnant women. Her blood pressure was higher than her doctor was comfortable with, and as a result she had been prescribed bed rest for the remaining two months of her pregnancy. It wasn't so much a serious problem as an annoying one.

Since her husband worked long hours, having her best friend, Brandy, around to help take care of her was priceless. Jen tried not to be too much of a burden on her friend—there's a fine line between letting someone help you and taking advantage of their generosity, and Jen didn't want to cross it.

Of all Jen's pregnancy symptoms and idiosyncrasies, her food cravings were the most pervasive and would come up at the strangest of times. Her cravings often overwhelmed her: the urge for shrimp cocktail was seemingly endless, only to be outdone by her constant need for Baskin-Robbins Peanut Butter 'n Chocolate ice cream. But Jen lived in a small town, and since both items were hard to find, she found herself begging her friend to stock up for her in the city.

Brandy loved helping her friend and often joked that Jen would have to reciprocate when the tables were turned—if Brandy got pregnant, she was going to demand peach cobbler at ten o'clock every night. But Jen was well aware that Brandy was going above and beyond the call of duty, coming in almost every day to see if Jen was all right and sometimes going as far as walking her to the shower.

During her last two weeks of pregnancy, Jen was feeling worse than ever. Brandy never failed to provide Jen with company, a shoulder to cry on, and of course, someone to run into town to pick up a box of Ding Dongs, a jar of pickles, or a bag of Cool Ranch Doritos. After Jen finally had her baby, she  did the only thing she could do to say thank you to the friend who had helped satisfy her constant needs: she named her baby daughter Brandy.

✿✿

*Our lives are shaped by
the friends we choose.*

Walking It Out

Janet and Carmen met as newlyweds living next door to one another, and a friendship quickly blossomed. As many friends do, they shared the highs and lows of their lives with each other, helping out as best they could.

After she had her first baby, Janet wanted to get back into shape. "Ugh. I still can't get back into my old pants," she complained, rubbing her belly. "I guess it's muumuu time for me. I never have time to exercise."

Carmen laughed. "You just had a baby! Tell you what—how about we start walking in the mornings together, before everyone's up."

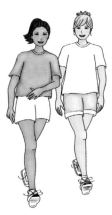

Janet agreed, and they set a routine. There were many days when hitting the snooze button was far more enticing, but the thought of letting each other down was enough of an incentive to lace up their shoes. Once out in the fresh air, the women were always glad they got up to greet the day—not only because the exercise was good for them, but because their deepening friendship was, too. Janet and Carmen walked together several times a week, and over the course of time, they went through many topics of discussion.

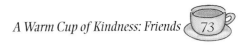

Once, at a cookout, Janet's husband asked the two women, "After all this time, what on earth do you two still find to talk about?"

Janet and Carmen just looked at each other. "Shoes!" Carmen laughed, winking at Janet. What she didn't add was that they also talked about everything from their own parents and children to their jobs, worries, hopes . . . and, of course, their husbands.

Over the years, the friends made accommodations for each other. When Carmen became pregnant, Janet slowed down her walking pace. Later, when Janet injured her leg and was trying to regain her strength, it was Carmen's turn to slow down. When Carmen was exhausted from visiting her mother in the hospital, Janet walked alone. And when Janet was having a difficult time at work and pleaded that she was too stressed to get up early, Carmen gently nudged her to resume their walks to reduce her stress.

What began as a simple effort toward well-being grew into a very special journey. In good times and in bad, they were literally walking through life together.

To be a friend you
must be there—
encouraging, cheering,
empathizing, crying.
It's all part of the
package.

The Friendship Connection

There's an old tradition of sharing a bread dough starter that's proven to be a wonderful way to connect with friends. Essentially, it involves making the ingredients for bread and splitting the dough to make Friendship Bread starter kits for a few friends, while enjoying your own delicious, freshly baked loaf. Think of it as a chain letter, but in bread form.

Each time I make my bread, my mind often wanders to my friends who will be receiving the starter kits. The thought of them preparing their own kits to share, and enjoying the process as I have, warms my heart.

As I knead the starter, I think of the bread and how it involves an entire chain of friendships around our town. I find it amazing that a simple (though delicious) loaf of bread can serve as a reminder of how connected we are to our friends.

PUMPKIN-PECAN FRIENDSHIP BREAD

3 cups chopped pecans, divided
1 can (16 ounces) solid-pack
   pumpkin
1 cup Starter (recipe follows)
4 eggs
½ cup vegetable oil
2 teaspoons vanilla
3 cups all-purpose flour

1 cup granulated sugar
1 cup packed light brown sugar
4 teaspoons ground cinnamon
2 teaspoons baking powder
1 teaspoon baking soda
1 teaspoon ground nutmeg
1 teaspoon ground ginger
1 teaspoon ground cloves

1. Preheat oven to 350°F. Grease and flour 2 (9½×4-inch) loaf pans. Set aside.

2. Reserve 1 cup pecans. Spread remaining 2 cups pecans in single layer in large baking pan. Bake 8 minutes or until golden brown, stirring frequently.

3. Combine pumpkin, Starter, eggs, oil, and vanilla in large bowl. Combine remaining ingredients in separate large bowl until well blended. Stir into pumpkin mixture just until blended. Stir in toasted pecans. Spoon batter evenly into prepared pans. Sprinkle reserved pecans evenly over batter.

4. Bake 1 hour or until toothpick inserted into center comes out clean. Cool in pans on wire rack 5 minutes. Remove from pans. Cool completely on wire rack. Wrap in plastic wrap. Store at room temperature up to 1 week. *Makes 2 loaves*

Starter

1 cup sugar
1 cup all-purpose flour
1 cup milk

1. Combine all ingredients in large resealable food storage bag. Knead bag until well blended. Let bag stand at room temperature 5 days. Knead bag 5 times each day.

2. On day 6, add another cup sugar, 1 cup flour, and 1 cup milk. Knead bag until well blended. Let stand at room temperature 4 days. Knead bag 5 times each day.

3. On day 10, pour 1 cup Starter into each of 3 bags. Reserve remaining 1 cup Starter for recipe. Give remaining bags of Starter with copy of recipe as gifts.

Contributing Writers

Rebecca Christian is a Des Moines–based writer, poet, and playwright who can be reached at rebecca.christian@mchsi.com.

Lain Ehmann is a California-based writer and mom to three.

Susan Farr Fahncke is founder of the inspirational Web site, www.2theheart.com. She can be contacted at susan@2theheart.com.

Marie D. Jones is the author of several nonfiction books and coauthor of more than three dozen inspirational books. She is an ordained minister.

Julie Clark Robinson is the award-winning author of *Live in the Moment* as well as the *General Hospital* Editor for Soaps.com. You can learn more about her at www.julieclarkrobinson.com.

Carol Stigger is a writer specializing in microcredit and poverty in developing countries. She works with a microcredit organization in India during the winter and lives in Italy every spring, writing travel articles and fiction.

Cover illustrations: Tina Dorman

Illustrators: Lynda Calvert-Weyant, Tina Dorman, Alyssa Hemsath-Mooney, Paula McArdle